STAGE 1

EXPLORE!

**BY JANICE PIMM, NARINDER DHAMI
AND SALLY PRUE**

**ILLUSTRATED BY ANDY ELKERTON,
BRIONY MAY SMITH, FREYA HARTAS,
CARLO MOLINARI AND QU LAN**

OXFORD
UNIVERSITY PRESS

CONTENTS

THE
MYSTERIOUS EGG

BY JANICE PIMM
ILLUSTRATED BY ANDY ELKERTON

BEFORE READING

Setting the scene

In this story, a boy makes an unusual and surprising discovery as he walks by the canal with his mum. He has to decide what to do with his mysterious find.

Prepare to read

Use the expert tips:

■ **Stop and check it makes sense – take action**
What do you think 'his mysterious find' might be?

■ **Read it again** Do you know where this story takes place and who is going to be in it? Read 'Setting the scene' (at the top of this page) again to make sure you spotted these details.

Challenge word

despair
Find this word on page 14. Can you work out what it means?

THE MYSTERIOUS EGG

Chapter 1

Jamie and his mum were getting ready to go for a walk by the canal. Jamie loved spotting the birds flying over the water.

"You're not going on another nature walk, are you?" asked Jamie's big brother, Ryan. "That's so boring. I'd rather play football any day!"

"Well, you don't need to come with us, Ryan," said Mum. Sometimes Jamie wished he and Ryan liked the same things.

Later, as Jamie and his mum walked along the canal bank, Jamie pointed to a grey heron.

"Look, Mum!" he said excitedly. "I think we'll spot lots of birds today."

Suddenly something caught Jamie's eye – a blue shape glittering in a bush. As Mum walked on, Jamie bent down and parted the branches. At the bottom of the bush was the most enormous egg Jamie had ever seen. It was bright blue with luminous silver speckles.

"Come on, Jamie!" called Mum. Jamie ran to catch up. He chatted to Mum as they walked along, but he couldn't get the egg out of his mind. What could it be? Where had it come from? It was far too big to be a bird's egg.

On the way back, Jamie felt excited when he saw the same bush again.

"I just need to tie my shoelace, Mum," he said. Mum walked on ahead. Jamie peered inside the bush, holding his breath. The mysterious egg was still there.

Jamie looked at the egg for a long time. He knew he should never pick up a bird's egg, but this one was different. It didn't have a nest and there didn't seem to be a mother bird anywhere. Anyway, it *wasn't* a bird's egg.

While Jamie stared, the egg began to rock gently from side to side. He couldn't believe his eyes. How was it moving? The egg rolled gently out of the bush on to the path and nudged Jamie's foot. He felt he was meant to pick it up.

Jamie quickly scooped up the egg and stuffed it into his rucksack. It was heavier than he'd imagined.

At home, Jamie hid the egg in his wardrobe, wrapped in a blanket. Every day when he got back from school, he rushed upstairs to see it. He stroked it when he woke up in the morning and before he went to sleep at night. He knew the egg was special – very special.

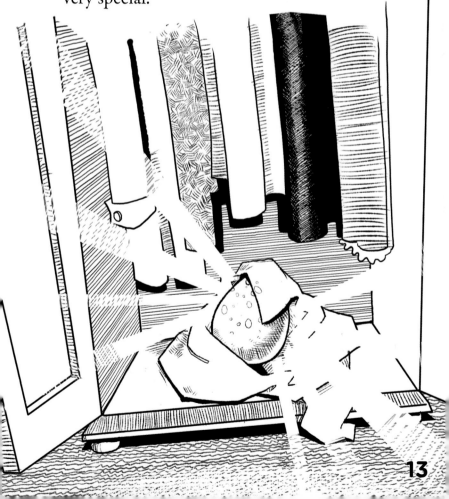

One day, Jamie got home from school, rushed upstairs and opened his wardrobe door. The egg had gone! All that was left was an empty blanket.

Jamie sat down on his bed in despair. He felt terribly lonely and sad inside. What had happened to his precious egg?

THE MYSTERIOUS EGG

Chapter 2

BEFORE READING

Prepare to read

You have already read Chapter 1. It will help you if you try to remember what happened before you start to read Chapter 2. What were the main events?

Use the expert tip:

- **Read it again** Jamie's worst moment came at the end of Chapter 1. Read page 14 again and think of words to describe his mood.

Challenge word

sneaky

Find this word on page 17. Can you work out what it means?

Chapter 2

Jamie sat in his bedroom, staring at the space in his wardrobe where his egg had been for so long. Just then, he heard a sneaky laugh from the room next door. He rushed into his brother's bedroom.

Ryan was sitting on his bed holding the precious blue egg.

"I knew you were hiding something," Ryan said. "What *is* this? It would make a great football!" Ryan tossed the egg into the air and caught it again.

Jamie couldn't bear to see his special egg in danger. He felt furious and frightened all at the same time.

"Give it back!" Jamie shouted, going red in the face. "Please don't break it ..."

Ryan just laughed. Jamie didn't want to snatch the egg in case it got broken. Tears stung his eyes.

"Let me have it," Jamie pleaded. "I need it."

Ryan was surprised to see how much his brother cared about the egg. He handed it back to Jamie.

"OK, you can have it," said Ryan. "It's only a stupid egg. If you think it's so special, you'd better look after it!"

Jamie held the egg close to his chest and carried it back to his room. Carefully, he wrapped it in the blanket.

"I'll always look after you," he whispered.

A few days later, Ryan came clattering downstairs while Jamie was watching television.

"Come quick, Jamie!" cried Ryan. "There's a tapping sound in your room."

The brothers raced upstairs. CRACK! A loud noise came from Jamie's bedroom ... and another. CRACK!

Jamie pulled open the wardrobe door. The egg was breaking.

"It's hatching!" cried Jamie.

A blue head peeked out. There was a tiny crest on the top of the head, and big eyes that were tightly shut.

One eye opened, then the other. The eggshell fell away to reveal a creature with four small legs, and silvery wings folded on its back. It was covered in blue, green and silver scales. A tiny wisp of smoke puffed from one of its nostrils.

"It's amazing!" said Jamie softly.

"It's a *dragon*!" said Ryan. "What are we going to do?"

The little creature tottered out of the wardrobe. Jamie picked it up.

"I'm going to look after it," said Jamie, hoping Ryan wouldn't tell Mum.

Ryan was silent for a while. Then he said, "I'd like to help you look after it. Can I?"

Jamie nodded, pleased Ryan was being friendly. The two boys grinned at each other. They were going to have a great time looking after their new pet!

Wildlife on Water

BY JANICE PIMM

BEFORE READING

Setting the scene

When you explore waterways around the world you can discover all sorts of interesting creatures. The wildlife could be in a British canal or as far away as the mighty Amazon River in South America.

Prepare to read

Think about other information texts you have read. What features do they have?

Look at the list below and skim through the text. Which features can you spot?

Features often found in an information text:
- Contents page
- Index
- Glossary
- Heading and sub-headings
- Labelled photos or diagrams
- Fact boxes

Challenge word

rarely
Find this word on page 32. Can you work out what it means?

Wildlife
on Water

Let's explore the wildlife on two very different waterways – a canal in Great Britain and the Amazon River in South America.

Britain's canals run through cities and countryside, and they are teeming with wildlife.

The Amazon rainforest is home to over 400 kinds of mammals, 300 reptiles, 1300 birds and 3000 freshwater fish **species**.

On the canal

If you take a walk along a canal path in Britain, these are some of the fascinating creatures you might spot.

Water vole

The water vole has a brown coat, a blunt nose and a round body. You might hear it before you see it. The first sign of a water vole is often a noisy plop! Look out for its burrows in canal banks.

small ears

Diet	stems and leaves of waterside plants
Size	12–20 cm with a tail of about 7 cm

Grey heron

The grey heron has long legs and an S-shaped neck. It stands perfectly still at the side of the water, watching out for fish. Quick as a flash, the heron will dart down to spear its **prey**.

long sharp bill

Diet	fish, reptiles, frogs, insects
Size	84–100 cm, wingspan 1.6–2 m

Kingfisher

The kingfisher is a **predator** that often catches fish bigger than itself. When it spots a fish, it dives into the water at lightning speed to catch its prey.

bright blue back

orange underneath

Diet	fish, tadpoles, insects
Size	length 16–17 cm, wingspan 24–26 cm

The Amazon River

The Amazon is one of the longest rivers in the world. These are some of the amazing creatures you might see there.

Anaconda

The anaconda is the heaviest snake in the world. This frightening predator lies still in the water, waiting for its prey. Then it wraps itself around its prey and squeezes until the prey cannot breathe.

dark pattern

Diet	fish, birds, deer, and even other anacondas
Size	length over 5 m, weight 97.5 kg

Black caiman

This huge reptile is the biggest predator in the Amazon but it rarely attacks humans. People are a bigger threat to the caiman than it is to them. It used to be hunted a lot, but now it is a protected species.

hard scales

70 sharp teeth

Diet	fish, birds, turtles, rodents, mammals
Size	length 4–6 m

Harpy eagle

If you're very lucky, you might spot a harpy eagle from the river. This fearsome predator is one of the largest, most powerful eagles in the world. Its talons can be as big as a bear's claws, and its legs can be as thick as a person's wrist.

hooked beak

grey face

massive talons

Diet	monkeys, sloths, baby deer, racoons, parrots
Size	length 90–100 cm, wingspan 2 m

Glossary

predator   an animal that hunts and kills another for food

prey   an animal that is hunted by another

species   a kind or type of animal or plant

Incredible Caves

BY NARINDER DHAMI

BEFORE READING

Setting the scene

Have you ever explored a cave? Have you ever wondered how caves came to exist? There are incredible caves in different parts of the world. Read this information text and discover some of their secrets.

Prepare to read

Look for features of information texts. How can you use these to help you understand what you are reading?

Use the expert tip:

- **Use text structures, features and language**

Do you know where to find one of the world's biggest caves? Turn to page 40 and read the caption on the photo.

Remember to read the captions as well as the main text to help you understand.

Challenge word

dense

Find the word on page 40. Can you work out what it means?

Incredible Caves

What is a cave?

Caves are hollow spaces underground or in the sides of hills or cliffs. It can take millions of years for a cave to form. So how does this happen?

How are caves formed?

Some caves are formed by water. When rainwater seeps through cracks in **limestone** rocks, it mixes with chemicals in the earth and becomes an **acid**. The acid then eats its way through the rocks, and holes appear. Over time, these holes grow bigger and bigger, and become caves.

Caves can also be formed in other ways.

Some caves are formed when big slabs of solid rock move apart.

Other caves are formed by strong waves hitting cliffs.

Some caves are caused by lava from volcanoes.

Son Doong

One of the world's biggest caves

The largest chamber in the Son Doong cave system is over 200m wide and is thought to be around 250m tall. It's difficult to visit Son Doong because it's a day and a half's trek from the nearest village, through the dense jungle.

Son Doong is in Vietnam and was discovered in 1991.

Crystal Cave

Discovered during a cricket game

Two boys were playing cricket when their ball disappeared down a hole. They discovered the hole was the entrance to an underground cave.

The landowner lowered his teenage son into the hole on a rope with only a bicycle lamp to light the darkness. He found a cave of amazing **stalactites** and **stalagmites**.

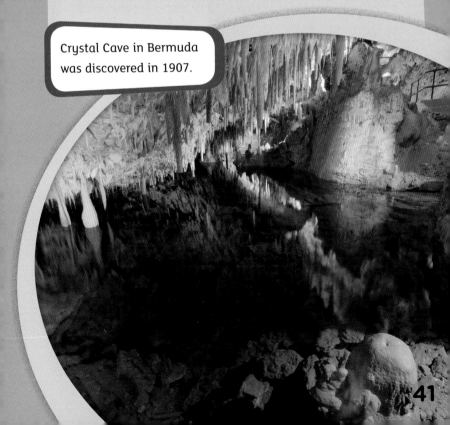

Crystal Cave in Bermuda was discovered in 1907.

Gough's Cave

The cave of secrets

The oldest complete human skeleton ever found in the British Isles was discovered in 1903 in Gough's Cave. The male skeleton, known as Cheddar Man, is thought to be around 9000 years old.

Gough's Cave is one of the Cheddar Caves in Somerset, England.

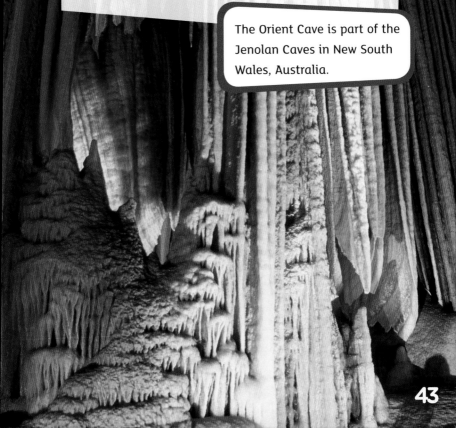

The Jenolan Caves

The world's oldest caves

The Jenolan Caves are around 340 million years old. The cave network is so large, it is still being explored. There are 40 km of passageways and more than 300 entrances. Some of the caves have spectacular rock formations, like the Orient Cave, seen here.

The Orient Cave is part of the Jenolan Caves in New South Wales, Australia.

Glossary

limestone   a type of rock, formed millions of years ago from layers of shells and coral

acid   a chemical that can dissolve hard substances

stalactite   an icicle-like pointed rock hanging from the roof of a cave

stalagmite   a cone-shaped pointed rock on the floor of a cave

DID YOU KNOW?

Here's how to remember the difference between stalactites and stalagmites:

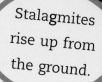

Stalactites hang from the ceiling.

Stalagmites rise up from the ground.

THE SECRET OF THE CAVE

BY NARINDER DHAMI

ILLUSTRATED BY BRIONY MAY SMITH

BEFORE READING

Setting the scene

Three friends, Ollie, Anka and Safeer, are on a school trip to a cave. They are supposed to be on a guided tour but Ollie has other ideas ...

Prepare to read

Pronoun activity: Improve this sentence by using the pronouns 'he' and 'his':
Ollie told Ollie's friends that Ollie thought that Ollie could climb up a stalactite.

Use the expert tip:

■ **Make connections – search for clues** Expert readers make connections between nouns and pronouns so that they know what each pronoun is referring to.

Challenge word

dismay – feeling worried or upset because something happened unexpectedly

Find this word on page 52. Read it in its sentence and check that you understand what it means.

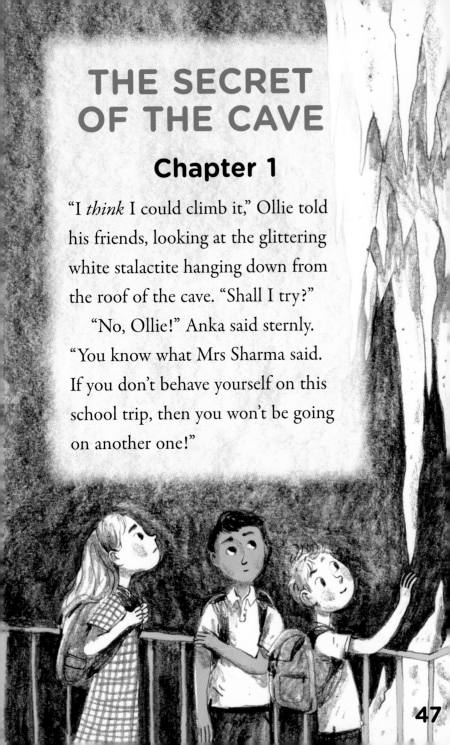

THE SECRET OF THE CAVE

Chapter 1

"I *think* I could climb it," Ollie told his friends, looking at the glittering white stalactite hanging down from the roof of the cave. "Shall I try?"

"No, Ollie!" Anka said sternly. "You know what Mrs Sharma said. If you don't behave yourself on this school trip, then you won't be going on another one!"

Ollie glanced over at their teacher and the rest of the class. They were listening to the guide explaining the history of the caves and how they'd been discovered.

"I bet I *could* climb that stalac-thingy if I tried," muttered Ollie.

"*Stalactite*," Anka said.

"And you're *not* climbing it."

"You already got into trouble with Mrs Sharma today, Ollie," Safeer reminded him.

"Just because I started eating my lunch early," Ollie grumbled.

"It was 9 am," Anka pointed out. "We hadn't even got on to the coach!"

"Whatever," Ollie replied, distractedly.

49

Ollie stared around the cave with interest. The stalactites and stalagmites were like something from outer space. Many of the rocks were fantastic, twisted shapes. "These caves are *amazing*."

"Maybe we should go and listen to the guide," Safeer suggested. "It'll really help us with our cave presentations when we're back at school."

"Hey," Anka said, suddenly realizing that the cave had gone very quiet. "Where's everyone gone?"

"Oh no!" Safeer gasped nervously. "What's Mrs Sharma going to say?"

"It's cool," Ollie replied with a grin. "I can still hear the guide talking. They went *this* way."

There were two winding rocky tunnels leading out of the cave, and Ollie led Anka and Safeer confidently down the right-hand one. To their dismay, the voice of the guide became fainter, not stronger.

"This isn't the right way," Anka said, frowning. "They must have taken the other exit, the left-hand one."

"Quick, let's go back!" Safeer said urgently. He was desperate to find the rest of the class before Mrs Sharma realized they were missing.

Anka and Safeer started back the way they'd just come, but then Anka stopped.

"Where's Ollie?" she asked, looking back over her shoulder.

"He's right behind us," Safeer replied, hurrying on.

"No, he isn't." Anka sounded worried. "Safeer, Ollie's vanished!"

THE SECRET OF THE CAVE

Chapter 2

BEFORE READING

Prepare to read

It will help your understanding if you remember what happened in Chapter 1 before you read Chapter 2. Where does the story take place? What were the main events?

Use the expert tips:

- **Predict**

- **Think and remember**
  - What is Ollie like?
  - What do you think has happened to Ollie?
  - What are his friends like?
  - What will his friends do next?

Make your predictions using what you already know about Ollie and his friends. Remember what you have read about what caves are like.

Challenge word

panicky
Find the word on page 59. Can you work out what it means?

Chapter 2

Anka and Safeer stared at each other in horror.

"Oh no!" Safeer whispered. "Ollie's lost. He could be anywhere in these caves."

"He's got to be around here somewhere!" Anka replied.

Anka noticed a long, narrow crack in the rockface. She went over and peered through it.

"Hello," said Ollie from the other side of the rock, making Safeer almost jump out of his skin. "I squeezed through the crack into this little cave. It's awesome."

"We've got to go!" Safeer wailed.

"All right," Ollie called. "I'm coming out."

"Come on, Ollie!" Anka said impatiently.

"This hole seems a lot narrower than when I got in," Ollie said in a panicky voice. "I don't think I can get out again."

"Pass us your backpack first," Anka suggested. "That might make it easier."

Ollie tried to shove his backpack through the hole, but, as usual, he hadn't fastened it properly. The backpack slipped and spilled its contents on to the ground – Ollie's lunchbox, his phone and all his money.

"Mrs Sharma's coming!" Safeer squealed.

Quickly, Ollie stuffed everything into his backpack. Scooping the last few coins off the ground, he shoved the backpack through the hole to Anka and then squeezed through himself. He was only halfway out when Mrs Sharma, the guide and the rest of the class appeared.

"Oliver Harris, what are you doing?" Mrs Sharma said in alarm.

Red in the face, Ollie wriggled out. In his hurry, he dropped the coins he still had in his hand. The guide picked them up.

"Where did you get this?" he asked Ollie, holding up a dirty, battered coin with a man's face on it.

Ollie couldn't understand why the guide sounded so excited. "It's not mine," he replied. "I must have picked it up in the cave back there."

"It's a very valuable coin," the guide said breathlessly. "It dates from the time when the Romans occupied Britain, over a thousand years ago. This is an extremely important discovery."

"I shall call the local museum and ask them to send someone to investigate," the guide went on. "There could be more coins hidden in that cave!"

"Cool!" Ollie gasped. A picture flashed into his head of a boy hiding his treasure in that cave, over a thousand years ago. A boy just like him.

Ollie couldn't wait to get back to school and write about it.

THE HOLIDAY HOVEL

BY SALLY PRUE
ILLUSTRATED BY FREYA HARTAS

BEFORE READING

Setting the scene

Jake, Holly and their mum have just arrived on an island for their summer holiday. But there will be no lazing on the warm beach or eating at restaurants on *this* island.

Prepare to read

Read the title and think about the word 'hovel'. What do you think a hovel is?

■ Explore vocabulary – clarify words and phrases

Turn to page 69, find the word 'hovel' and read the first four sentences. Were you right about what a hovel is?

■ Visualize – form a picture in your mind

Imagine what the 'holiday hovel' looks like.

- What is it made from?

- Are there signs that it is tumbling down?

- What would it be like to sleep in?

Challenge word

floundering

Find the word on page 72. Can you work out what it means?

THE HOLIDAY HOVEL

"*This* isn't a holiday island!" exclaimed Jake wildly.

Jake and Holly climbed off the boat on to the shore and looked round in dismay. Mum had chosen this place for their summer holiday, but there was no sign of any houses or roads. It was all just ... *rocks*.

"There's nothing here!" Holly wailed.
"We thought it would be like last year! With
shops! Clubs!"

"Go-cart racing!" added Jake.

"We'll go exploring instead," said Mum
happily. "We'll gather seaweed for dinner."

"We'll get poisoned!" howled Holly.

"Where are we staying?" asked Jake
nervously.

"Let's go and find out!" said Mum, taking
out a map and striding off uphill.

The holiday home was basically a shed. It had bunk beds, a table, some chairs and a camping cooker.

"Holiday home? This is a holiday *hovel*!" said Holly, outraged.

"Where's the toilet?" asked Jake worriedly.

"Oh, we dig our own," said Mum.

She picked up a book labelled 'Instructions for Cooker' and flicked through it.

"We'll worry about dinner later," she decided. "Come on, let's explore!"

Mum strode along happily in her new walking boots.

"Look at those fantastic rain clouds!" she said.

"Great," muttered Holly. "We're going to get soaked. We'll probably catch colds and die."

Mum ignored her.

"Isn't exploring *marvellous*?" she said, marching down the track.

Jake watched Mum go.

"That path looks really boggy," he observed. "I hope we don't get stuck."

Mum turned and waved.

"Isn't it fabulous? I'm so glad we – *aaarrrggghhhh*!"

Mum's scream echoed round the hill as she tripped over a rock and fell backwards out of sight.

"Where's she gone?" gasped Jake.

"Quick!" shouted Holly, and they ran down the track.

Mum had been lucky: she'd landed in a pool of deep soft mud.

She was covered in it.

"Help!" she shouted, floundering. "I can't get out!"

She took off her coat, and they used it as a rope to rescue her.

"How will you get *clean*?" asked Holly. "There's no shower."

"You'll have to wash in the sea," suggested Jake.

Mum squelched to the sea and waded in – and then at last Jake and Holly could laugh.

"Now Mum will be as keen to leave this awful island as we are," said Holly with satisfaction.

It was cold and dark when they got back.

"I'm afraid we'll have to go home," Jake told Mum, when they got back to the Holiday Hovel. "This place is too dangerous for us to stay."

Mum suddenly started laughing.

"Go home?" she said, dripping all over the floor. "Of course not. It's fantastic! I can't *wait* to see which of us falls in the mud tomorrow!"

Two Great Explorers

BY SALLY PRUE

ILLUSTRATED BY CARLO MOLINARI

BEFORE READING

Setting the scene

You would expect explorers to travel to faraway places, but some explore much closer to home. Find out about two very different explorers – one who travelled over 6000 miles from Germany to South America and another who just went a few steps into her garden in England.

Prepare to read

Did anything surprise you when you read the 'Setting the scene' paragraph?

Use the expert tip:

■ **Ask a question** I wonder how you can be an explorer in your own garden?

Make up a question of your own about this text. See if you can answer your question as you are reading.

Challenge word
inspired
Find this word on page 80. Can you work out what it means?

Two Great Explorers

Alexander von Humboldt and Jennifer Owen are great explorers who explored the world in very different ways.

Jennifer Owen

Alexander von Humboldt

Alexander von Humboldt

Alexander von Humboldt wanted to be an explorer, but his strict mother disapproved. When she died, Alexander inherited enough money to pay for his travels. He sailed to South America, and was suddenly surrounded by wonderful things.

Alexander saw oilbirds that could **navigate** pitch-black caves by listening to the echoes of the clicks they made, rather like bats do.

oilbirds

He saw electric eels, which killed his horses as they waded across the Orinoco River. Instead of being scared off, Alexander became fascinated by electricity.

On Mount Chimborazo, Alexander climbed to a world record-breaking **altitude**.

Everywhere Alexander went he recorded the **climate**, the rocks and the wildlife. He was interested in everything, even bird poo (it made good fertilizer).

electric eel

Alexander wanted to know how the whole world worked. He became very famous, and his discoveries inspired other scientists to travel and explore the world.

Alexander's namesakes

Many animals have been named after Alexander von Humboldt including the Humboldt penguin, the Humboldt squid, Humboldt's river dolphin and Humboldt's hog-nosed skunk. Lots of plants and trees, mountains and mountain ranges, and a river and glacier – to name just a few – also bear his name.

Humboldt's hog-nosed skunk

Jennifer Owen

Jennifer Owen proved that someone can be an explorer without leaving home.

Although she grew up in the UK, Jennifer spent some time living in Africa. She noticed that her garden contained more types of insect than the surrounding countryside. When she returned home to England she decided to explore the wildlife of her medium-sized garden in the city of Leicester.

Jennifer saw urban foxes in her Leicester garden.

What can you discover in an ordinary city garden? Well, Jennifer found seven **mammals**, 54 **species** of bird and nearly 2000 different types of insect.

Insects and spiders

Jennifer found 375 types of moth, 59 types of bee, 62 types of wasp, 422 types of beetle and 80 types of spider in her ordinary garden.

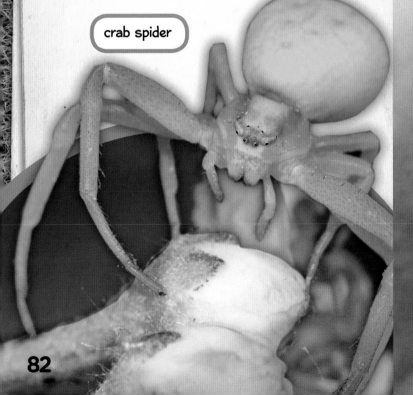

crab spider

Altogether, Jennifer found 2673 types of plants and animals in thirty years. Twenty had never been seen in Britain before, and seven were completely new to science. Even so, her guess is that she failed to spot *most* of the wildlife in the garden (she didn't see a housefly!). It is likely that the true total might be nearer 8000.

orange ladybird

Alexander von Humboldt travelled across the world making new discoveries, and Jennifer Owen made exciting discoveries in her own garden. Her important study has proved that even ordinary places can be very extraordinary indeed.

Glossary

altitude   height above sea level

climate   the sort of weather that a place has

mammal   an animal that feeds its young on milk

navigate   to find your way

species   a type of animal or plant – for example, house sparrow and red kite are species of bird.

THE REINDEER PATH

BY SALLY PRUE
ILLUSTRATED BY QU LAN

BEFORE READING

Setting the scene

In the lands close to the Arctic, people have lived alongside herds of reindeer for thousands of years. Every year, people who take care of the reindeer – the reindeer herders – travel with the herd as the animals migrate hundreds of miles to their summer and winter feeding grounds.

However, deep below that same ground there is oil to be found. When big machines arrive to drill for oil, the reindeer can be scared away and may not reach their vital supplies of food.

Prepare to read

What might stop reindeer from travelling to their usual feeding places?

Challenge word

hesitated – stopped uncertainly for a moment

Find the word on page 90. Read it in its sentence and check you understand what it means.

THE REINDEER PATH

Rob and his uncle Sam usually enjoyed spending time together, but today Uncle Sam was fed up.

Sam's job was exploring for oil. "There's trouble at the new oilfield," he told Rob, putting away his phone. "Someone's smashed up some machinery in the night."

"Who would do that?" asked Rob.

"Criminals hired by another oil company," explained his uncle. "If they can cause an oil spill then our company will get thrown off the site. Then their company can take it over. Look, Rob, I'm going to have to fly up there. I can't leave you here alone, so you'll have to come with me."

"To an oilfield?" said Rob. "In a helicopter? Brilliant!"

***

The oilfield was scattered with cabins, trucks and machinery. It was spring, but an icy Arctic wind whipped around Rob and Sam.

"Have a look round, Rob," said his uncle. "I shouldn't be long."

Rob went to talk to a man stacking some pipes.

"Did you hear the criminals smashing things up last night?" Rob asked.

The man hesitated. "The wind was howling too loudly to hear anything much," he said.

"Oh, so that's why they chose such bad weather for their raid," said Rob, shivering.

The man laughed.

"This is *good* weather for round here," he said. "But then I'm used to this place. My family have been reindeer herders here since long before I was born."

"There are reindeer? Here?"

"There won't be, once the noisy drilling starts," the man said sadly. "This oilfield will block their spring migration route."

Rob looked round. "The drilling will be bad for your family, then," he said.

"Rob!" called Uncle Sam. "Time to go!"

Sam and Rob walked to the helicopter with the oil worker.

"This attack is a real mystery," said Sam. "No outsiders have been seen anywhere nearby."

Rob had been thinking hard.

"Uncle Sam, did you know this site will block a reindeer migration route?" he asked. "It's going to affect all the reindeer herders."

"Really?" said Sam thoughtfully. "So that means that other oil companies aren't the only people who might want to stop us drilling here. The reindeer herders will also want us to stop."

Rob nodded.

Sam turned to the oil worker. "Do you think people would stop smashing up our machinery if we moved the drilling site across the lake?" he asked.

The man grinned. "You know," he said, "I think they would."

On the ride home Rob
saw thousands of reindeer
travelling north.

He was glad there was
room for the reindeer herders,
as well as for the oilfield.